AMAZING MOSAIC
COLOR-BY-NUMBERS

AMAZING MOSAIC
COLOR-BY-NUMBERS
REVEAL BEAUTIFUL IMAGES SQUARE BY SQUARE AS YOU COLOR

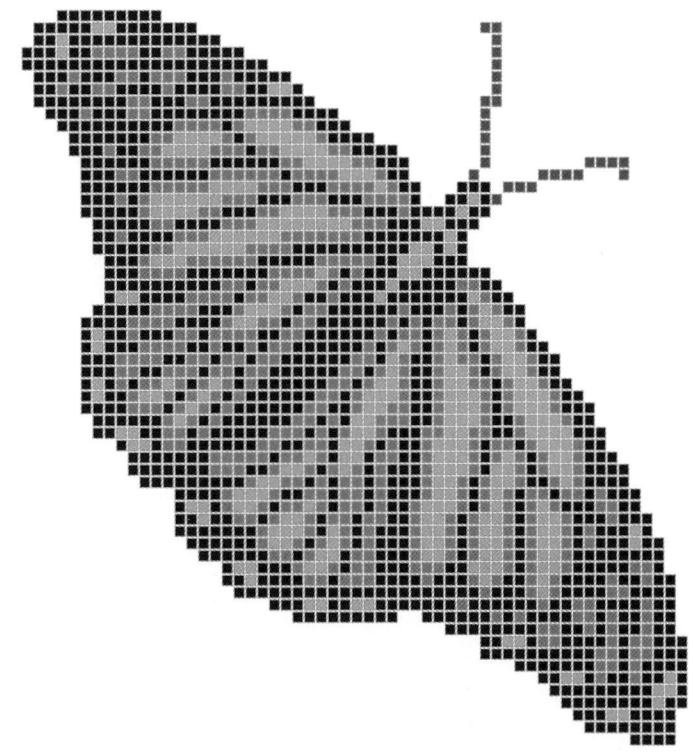

GEORGIE FEARNS & DIEGO VAISBERG

SIRIUS

SIRIUS

This edition published in 2023 by Sirius Publishing, a division of
Arcturus Publishing Limited,
26/27 Bickels Yard, 151–153 Bermondsey Street,
London SE1 3HA

ISBN: 978-1-3988-3045-5
CH011267NT

Printed in China

INTRODUCTION

Welcome to the fascinating world of mosaic coloring by numbers. Each image is divided into hundreds of tiny squares, each of which has been allocated a number that equates to a color. Before you start to color, the shape and form of the picture is very hard to detect, so there's an enjoyable mystery to be revealed as you fill in the squares to reveal what they add up to.

There's a wonderful selection of different images to choose from, including a sumptuous range of foods from sundaes to sushi, famous features such as the Great Wall of China and the Statue of Liberty, as well as birds and animals from the glorious flamingo and hummingbird to delightful portraits of cats and dogs. There is also a range of patterns, including a tricky leopard print as a special challenge.

For a fun way to concentrate and relax, just take a selection of colored pencils, choose an image to focus on, and while away a couple of hours revealing the mystery within the mosaic.